HOMO SAPIENS

Copyright © 2020
University Press
All Rights Reserved

Table of Contents

Introduction
Chapter 1: Humble Beginnings
Chapter 2: Cognitive Revolution
Chapter 3: The Agricultural Revolution
Chapter 4: Mankind on the Seas
Chapter 5: Establishing Human Hierarchies
Chapter 6: First Known Writings
Chapter 7: Religion
Chapter 8: Learning to Work Together
Chapter 9: The Rise of Capital
Chapter 10: Empires
Chapter 11: Enlightenment
Chapter 12: Science
Chapter 13: Capitalism
Chapter 14: The Industrial Revolution
Chapter 15: The Digital Revolution
Chapter 16: Familial Structures
Chapter 17: Humanity's Future
Conclusion

Introduction

With more than 7.5 billion people in the world occupying all seven continents, humans are among the more prolific and mobile creatures on Earth. However, they have fairly humble beginnings. The history of humanity is long and unexpected. The species Homo sapiens was not the first species of sapiens, but we are now the only remaining species. With our soft, bare bodies and lack of natural weapons, humans are a unique species that learned to rely on their brains and each other over their natural physical prowess.

There is no other creature that has been able to travel the world with so little - other than imagination. There is little evidence that any other animal is capable of such thinking, and no other creatures base their daily routines on something as abstract as money. Humans tend to see this as a sign of intellectual superiority, but there are no other species that suffer from the kinds of mental health issues that plague modern humans.

How did we get here? And what can our past tell us about our future? Human history is short compared with many other animals. Scientists, archeologists, and historians study the beginnings of human history to help predict where the species is going, including its possible evolution into something else entirely.

Chapter 1

Humble Beginnings

Homo sapiens is the species to which all modern human beings belong. Homo is Latin for "human." Sapien is Latin for "wise." So, a homo sapien is literally a "wise human." People walking around the Earth today are all classified as Homo sapiens, but we are not the only species under the homo classification. In fact, we aren't even the first species to come under this classification. Chronologically, it is thought that humanity, as we know it today - Homo sapiens - is simply the latest version of the classification. Our species is thought to have evolved about 10,000 years ago. However, the Homo classification goes back about 2.5 million years with the species called Australopithecus.

It is thought that Australopithecus originated in Africa. Restless, they soon migrated to other continents, including Europe and Asia. Because various groups lived in significantly different environmental conditions, the species evolved differently on the three primary continents.

Though these species died off relatively quickly compared to the others, there were also a few unique evolutions in remote locations.

The Australopithecus that moved east evolved into Homo Erectus, which translates to man upright. This species has the longest record of existence - about 2 million years.

Two known species of Homo evolved in Europe.

- The Australopithecus that settled in most of Europe evolved into Homo neanderthalensis, or Man from the Neander Valley. Because they lived in much colder climates than the other species, they became larger and heavier to survive the colder conditions. However, they were not the species that lived in the most extreme colds.

- The Australopithecus that moved into the extreme northern parts of Europe evolved into Homo Denisova. Not much is known about this classification as the remains of the first specimen were uncovered in Siberia during 2010.

At least two different species evolved on remote islands.

- Some Australopithecus moved onto a remote island known today as Java. With their very different survival needs, these remote Australopithecus evolved into Homo Solensis, which translates to Solo Valley man.
- Near the island of Java is another series of islands that saw the evolution of Homo Floresiensis, the smallest of the Homo species.

The Australopithecus that initially remained in Africa evolved into several different species:

- Homo rudolfensis, or man of Lake Rudolf
- Homo ergaster, or man working
- Homo sapiens

Each region saw the rise of different types of Homo because of the extreme differences in environmental conditions. This is noticeable from the very different skeletal frames that remain today. What is universal is that they all had a larger brain proportionate to their weak frames. Those larger brains required a lot more energy to survive, and survival was much harder as they did not have the kinds of natural weaponry that other animals had.

There were two significant advantages to those larger brains, which were possible because all of the different Homo species walked upright. This allowed their bodies to better distribute their weight. It also meant that their hands were free to do other things. From hunting and gathering to fighting, the erect position of the Homo body allowed them to do more than any other species. The larger brain also allowed for a different type of thinking, particularly in terms of problem-solving.

For women, the shift to walking on two legs was detrimental to furthering the population, though. Using only two legs instead of four meant that their bodies had to evolve to balance better, and that meant that the size of women's hips shrank. As a result, even today, natural childbirth (without the aid of medical professionals) for humans is the most dangerous and potentially deadly of any animal on Earth.

It is thought that Homo sapiens first started controlling fire about 800,000 years ago. Homo erectus and Neanderthals also appear to have been proficient in using this unique tool. Fire became a way for the fragile Homo species to protect themselves, but it also gave them warmth. Over time, they realized that it could be used to cook food, a discovery that worked better with the sensitive human digestive system.

About 70,000 years ago, sapiens became restless and began to spread across the continents, just as the Australopithecus had before them. Around this time, the other species seem to have started dying off. There are two primary theories on what happened to the other species.

The Interbreeding Theory has Homo sapiens mating with the other species - a theory largely backed up by DNA evidence. Some scientists today say that we are not entirely Homo Sapiens, but a mix of Homo sapiens, Homo erectus, and Homo neanderthals.

The Replacement Theory suggests that Homo sapiens largely killed off the other species. According to this theory, Homo sapiens committed genocide of our closest related species.

What happened was likely a combination of the two explanations, just as explorers have done in more recent history (the last few hundred years).

Chapter 4

Mankind on the Seas

Homo sapiens have been restless ever since they left Africa, and they spread much further than most people today realize. They spread across Europe and Asia, simply walking across the lands and exploring. However, they did not just move across the land. Long before Europeans took to the water, Homo sapiens from Asia, using boats that they had built (thanks to the Cognitive Revolution), set off from the southern parts of Asia and headed toward the many islands to the south. Over time, they continued to travel the waters to other regions where none of the other homo species had been. It is thought that the first significant venture from the three continents occurred around 450,000 years ago, and the first place they went to was Australia and the surrounding islands. Humans were the first to make such a long trip across water without thousands of years of evolution – like whales and dolphins.

It is thought that these early adventurers arrived in larger numbers, establishing communities upon their arrival. However, this is a guess as their boats, oars, and other tools have never been found. The boats and tools, if and when they existed, were made of organic materials that could not survive hundreds of thousands of years intact.

One of the reasons histories and archeologists estimate that the trip or trips were about 450,000 years ago is because there was a very sudden change in the animal life at about that time. Australia used to have more than 20 large species of animals, including kangaroos that were over six feet tall, as well as an incredibly unique lion that was a marsupial. There is a wealth of jokes about the kinds of strange and dangerous creatures that live in Australia today, but there were far more when humans arrived. Many of the animals started dying off after humans arrived, presumably because they were hunted to extinction. This is a pattern that is not unique just to Australia. A similar wave of extinction occurred at about the time historians think that humans started to arrive in North and South America. Larger animals would have been easy to spot, making them better targets for hunters. Since the animals had had no previous exposure to the small, non-threatening looking humans, the animals did not learn to be afraid of them. Larger animals have a longer gestation period and tend to have fewer babies since they usually are much harder to kill, so they have fewer natural predators. The large animals did not have time to learn to fear and escape humans before they were wiped out.

Based on skeletal remains and the waves of extinction, it appears that Homo sapiens killed about half of all the large land mammals long before humans learned to write, or even before they created the wheel. It is a significant downside to the spread of people across the globe, and it is a problem that occurred several more times in human history.

Humans had learned how to navigate the waters, but they had not yet established how to establish a balance with their new environments. It could be argued that it is a balance we still do not know how to establish.

Chapter 5

Establishing Human Hierarchies

For most of human history, we have lived in groups, but it was only after the Agricultural Revolution that we started to develop hierarchies. We do not have records (writing had not yet been established, and cave paintings did not include hierarchies) when hierarchies started to develop or evolved. There are many theories, but there is some undeniable evidence that indicates when those hierarchies were not only fully formed, but the evidence seems to make it far more evident than any kind of writing.

This evidence of human hierarchical evolution is most easily recognizable in the form of pyramids. Based on these massive structures, it was clear that humans had already formed their hierarchies, and those hierarchies had become incredibly large. Creating pyramids is not an easy task, and based on the periods when we do have writings about pyramids, we have an idea of what those hierarchies were.

Of course, the kind of hierarchy that was large enough to create pyramids was not a system that could come into being in a few months or even a few years. It was a type of community that took hundreds of years to form.

It is thought that people began to settle in and around established farms as they started to give up their nomadic lifestyles. This could have helped to contribute to those early hierarchies. The farmers who already knew how to plant and harvest would have had more power over the newer settlers. They would have lived in small homes, with families living separately instead of with a large group. This new change in behavior likely led to people developing a greater sense of self. They almost certainly became more individualistic during this time, which typically contributes to people being more selfish and self-seeking.

With this new shift in focus from the group to individuals, it would become clear that there needed to be rules to dissuade people from acting on their more selfish desires. As settlements grew and attracted more people, it would also be clear that there needed to be more structure. This would lead to rules and the need for enforcers and judges, as well as taxes to provide financial support for those new positions. Of course, these new structures probably had a minimal resemblance to today's complex structures, but they were a start down the path to creating increased social order. With such a structure in place, there is always a group or individual at the top. As Homo sapiens tamed the world around them, they began to structure themselves.

Settling down also came with a whole host of new worries that humans did not have before the Agricultural Revolution. Humans had always been aware of the seasons, changing their movements to be in the right places for food, water, and shelter. Now they were tied to a single place. This made them far more reliant on the food they grew. If the seasons did not follow the same patterns of the past, particularly during floods or droughts, entire communities could be wiped out since people would not have the food they needed to survive.

All of this happened around the time when people started to put their faith in deities. The settlements started to be banded together by their shared concerns and the belief structures that they formed. They became more willing to buy into beliefs, including in the hierarchies.

People became more individualistic on some levels, but they also began to feel a greater bond to their settlements. After all, if the crops failed, it could kill all of them, not just a few people. This would explain why people were willing to belong on a lower tier of the hierarchy. The people at the top had more privileges, but they also had more responsibility to the people of the community. This belief system made it easier for its followers to pay taxes and follow laws. The community would have men who were paid to protect them and people to protect them from lawlessness within the settlement. Over time, taxes went to improvements like roads and other community projects that benefited everyone, not just a few people. A thousand years later, Rome became an example of just how much taxes can do. Taxes paid for innovations, like water systems, and massive entertainment areas, such as amphitheaters and colosseums. This was still a long way in the future from when the first pyramids were built, but it shows how those early settlements evolved into large, complex social, governmental, and hierarchical systems.

Chapter 6

First Known Writings

When we think about the first writings, we imagine that the writers were writing stories, histories, or even laws. In reality, the first writings were far less interesting, and they did not involve words. The records that were needed related to the growing amounts of data accumulated as societies became more complex. The growing hierarchies and ability to justify those hierarchies required tracking the number of people, the amount of food, number of warriors, taxes collected, and other types of numeric information. After a certain size, trying to remember all of that data was pretty much impossible. Writing became necessary because of the limits of the human brain.

1. Our memories are limited. One can only retain so much information, even if that information is presented in pictures. Writing it down made tracking much more accurate.

2. Even if we could remember everything, people do not live forever. When one of the accountants died, all of the data stored in that person's mind was gone. Having a record made it easier to track, regardless of if the person died or moved on to do something else.

3. Numbers are far more difficult to retain than images and concepts. Our ability to retain numbers is far less reliable. This is best seen by the types of earliest writings that used images to depict what was being recorded.

The earliest type of writing appeared in Mesopotamia - devised by the Sumerians before 3000 BCE. Given how large the civilization was, the Sumerians needed writing to maintain their military, tax system, and a vast array of records. The records from this period are just as dull as one would expect. Scribes would have recorded the details, showing what was considered significant. While it was important at the time, it does not make for a very engaging read.

The writings of the Sumerians are the ones that we often study, but writing was developed in other places around the world, although the timelines are less well-known. For example, The Incan Empire was recording similar details an ocean away, and they did not have any kind of contact with the people back in Europe, Asia, and Africa. They had the same inspiration and need to record data as other humans all over the world as their civilizations grew. It was quite a shock to the Spanish explorers who arrived and found the Incans using quipus. These were colorful knots on cords that represented different kinds of numbers. It was so effective that the Spanish adapted it to keep their own books.

Writing has changed and evolved. People realized that it could do more than just record numbers and data. The Egyptians created hieroglyphics to tell stories about their leaders. The Chinese had their own unique type of writing that evolved into the very complicated characters used today.

Civilizations began to develop more complicated characters and methods of recording more complex ideas, particularly about their own histories and religions. Arabic numerals had a significant effect on writing in northern Africa, the Middle East, and Europe. The specific development of numbers representing a type of data allowed for more efficient writings that could be used almost universally. The Arab civilizations were not the only ones to develop numbers, but they popularized their system and refined it in a way that no other civilization could duplicate. Part of the popularity of Arabic numerals was that each number was distinctive such that it was hard to confuse one number for another. They were so refined that we still use distinct numerals today.

Chapter 7

Religion

Religion is a difficult subject to discuss because it usually inspires strong emotional responses. One of the primary purposes of religion is to bring people together under a common belief system. However, that has also proven to be part of the problem as it is often used to create tensions that may not otherwise have been present.

The earliest records of religion show how religions were used to help keep people in line, based on what the people at the top of the social hierarchy wanted. Fictions were created to justify the authority of the people who remained at the top. This fiction would change when a new person or group rose to power. The early religions began to make inequality a part of the nation; it was a tool to try to retain the status quo. For example, The Code of Hammurabi was a basic code of conduct and social structure in Babylonia around 1750 BCE. According to the Code, the rulers were speaking for their gods,

Chapter 2

Cognitive Revolution

What differentiated the Homo sapiens from the other primary species, Homo erectus and Homo neanderthals, was that they were better at problem-solving. While the other species had control of the resources in the beginning, Homo sapiens learned from their losses when they were struggling for power. They likely devised new ways to gain control until they finally proved to be successful.

This came to be known as the Cognitive Revolution, which occurred anywhere from 70,000 to 30,000 years ago. Homo sapiens began making more complicated tools, such as lamps, boats, and bows and arrows. As a result of these changes, their language became more complicated to get across their more complex ideas. They started to provide more detailed warnings about things they had seen or places where they had found better resources. This allowed them to return with larger numbers to collect items that they wanted or to avoid potential dangers entirely. Homo sapiens became more social, and it likely around this time that they began to gossip as that information could be useful for survival. People learned to cooperate and work more like a collective body, which allowed for them to move around in larger groups.

During this time, people began to think in more abstract terms, with concepts like justice and creativity becoming a growing interest among the larger communities. While similar animals like chimpanzees have groups of between 25 and 50 members, humans can have groups of up to 150 people and still know about each individual within the community. That is because humans developed the ability to describe and define people based on what they knew about each individual. Though we cannot possibly know all of the members of most religions, fandoms, or organizations (they tend to have hundreds of thousands to millions of members), we have things in common with these groups, all because of abstract ideas.

The Cognitive Revolution changed how people thought, and that gave rise to religions, organizations, governments, and empires later on. Along with the ability to build communities apparently out of nothing more than an idea, it also made those communities vulnerable, as was aptly demonstrated by the French Revolution. When people within a community cease to believe in the belief structure (in that case, the French monarchy and government), the community collapses. Nations and empires have had increasingly shorter periods of control, the more recent they are. The Spanish Empire lasted hundreds of years, while the British Empire lasted over 100 years.

The most significant difference between the beginning and the end of the Cognitive Revolution was the reliance on language and history over biological necessities. Humans started to be swayed by ideas to do things that may have been against their immediate needs, something that no other animal does.

Chapter 3

The Agricultural Revolution

By the time the Cognitive Revolution was ending, Homo sapiens had begun to look at the world differently. They had already domesticated canines, and it appears that this was done simultaneously in Europe and Asia, showing how easily adaptable canines are to humans' needs. Apart from dogs, though, humans had not domesticated any other animals, instead opting to hunt them. Dogs were easy to take with them as they roamed the different terrains. Taking care of herds and flocks of animals was far too difficult for people of the time.

While they had started to establish beliefs, they likely were not complicated because humans were still having to fight each other over limited resources. Governments were not really possible, nor were there any complicated religious structures as nomads with a particular belief system not shared by others could be wiped out by a bad winter. This would destroy the entire belief system. Groups were continually being defeated and merged into other bands.

Foraging for food began to teach people more about the different climates and which plants were easy to grow. Over time, this knowledge grew into a better understanding of the regions and what kind of desirable plants could thrive in them. This developed into a desire to plant and control the lands so that people could feed themselves more easily.

About 30,000 years ago, the Agricultural Revolution began, and it was a significant trade-off from the previous way people lived. As long as the weather was good, the food supply was more certain. However, working the lands was much harder on the human body, and humans had to adapt a different schedule to work the lands. Taking care of children became much harder as the adults had to split their time between childcare and farming. Child mortality and physical ailments resulting in death increased.

It is thought that during this period, religions began to form, primarily based on animism, or the belief that all plants and animals have a spirt. Humans began to farm the lands, but they still primarily hunted and fished for their meat. The belief in animism reflected the human reliance on the land to survive. Cave paintings seem to indicate early human animism.

Apart from the remaining relics that indicate that humans were beginning to farm the lands and the cave paintings that are entirely up to individual interpretation, there is not much left from this period in the history of Homo sapien.

which justified all of the laws and decrees of the rulers. In many ancient kingdoms, most notably ancient Greece, religion justified slavery and class by saying that it was part of the way the gods intended things to be. Religion is not the only type of social structure that has justified inequality, with systems like capitalism still doing it today. According to capitalism, someone who is successful must have more skills or ability than those who do not succeed. Some cases support this, but about as many that do not. Similarly, at its core, communism is supposed to mean equality for everyone, but the examples of communism are often more like dictatorships because the governments put some people at the top, which is, by definition, unequal from those they rule. There is a tendency in any larger society to develop some amount of inequality to maintain the norm.

A familiar word comes from a similar kind of societal justification of inequality: "outcast." The origin of the word comes from the Hindi caste system that specified how people were meant to interact with people in different classes within that system. Those who were at the top of the caste system would minimize their interaction with people of lower classes, and those classes were based on a person's birth. People were not allowed to marry outside of their caste and often did not socialize with others not in their caste. People who were born outside of that system were outcasts, and they were considered the lowest group, with peasants being considered higher than the outcasts.

This kind of system structure was fairly universal across the globe. Many rulers aligned themselves with their gods to quell any dissatisfaction with the system, which had limited success. Perhaps the most notable overthrow of such a belief in the rulers' divinity was the French Revolution in which the people decided that the injustices were too grave to be something that their deity would allow.

Religion has been used to justify other kinds of inequality, such as against different races, religions, and women.

While many negatives can be attributed to religion, there are at least as many positives about it. People have used religion to appeal to others' compassion and to unite them during difficult times. During the Middle Ages, the church was often the most active authority in helping and teaching peasants while lords and ladies indulged in their privileges.

The primary difference between the positives and negatives is that the negatives tend to be easier to identify than the positives. This could be because there is an expectation for religion to be beneficial, so when it is used to benefit others, it does not receive as much attention. Religion can make people feel better during difficult times and provides a sense of community as much as division. It is more of a quiet form of positivity that tends to provide relief and a sense of

community instead of trying to dictate the secular world.

Chapter 8

Learning to Work Together

Why have people sacrificed and worked together - sometimes to their own personal detriment? It seems they were willing to trade freedom for security. Over time, the agreement to accept limits allows people to work in increasingly larger groups.

Living in towns and cities is another way in which people agree to accept limitations based on a mutually beneficial agreement. This was not something that happened overnight. The Cognitive Revolution helped to make this kind of acceptance possible as people were able to rationalize a change when it improved their chance of survival. It allowed for people to believe in different ideologies and intangible concepts, then to form different kinds of cultures and civilizations. Globalization is a significant example of this. We have accepted certain truths and agreements, which allow us to interact with people worldwide.

The drive to feel connected has grown over time. When people first began to settle down and form larger groups, they made up a small percentage of the population. By the 5th century, more commonly called the Middle Ages, an estimated 90% of humanity lived in some kind of civilization. Another way to consider this is to think that 700 years ago, less than 10% of humanity did not live in an extensive network.

Problems tend to arise when it becomes clear that certain parts of the societal agreement are not being upheld. The repeated unrest in the United States since the 1960s shows how Americans have certain expectations of how they will be treated based on the physical agreement called *The Constitution*. The French Revolution, World War II, and many other instances of significant unrest are examples of the sense of an agreement being breached, and humans have thousands of years of history showing what happens when one part of a societal agreement is not met.

Chapter 9

The Rise of Capital

Humans are the only creatures that place significant value on another concept – capital. Other animals may steal items like ribbons and shiny objects, but their value is not the same as that of humanity's currency and capital. No other species today naturally barters and trades the way we do, unless they have been taught to by people. Animals like chimpanzees have been taught how to use currency, but it is not an idea that they came up with on their own.

The Agricultural Revolution marked the beginning of the idea that items could be traded. From that humble beginning rose trade and the bartering of goods.

Trading food was where it began, but, over time, it became cumbersome and problematic. Many foods go bad after a certain amount of time, which meant that trade was usually restricted to small regions. If many settlements grew the same foods, there was not much to trade.

However, there could be other goods that were of value in bartering.

The idea of currency is a concept that existed nearly everywhere that humans have settled. Many native peoples used currencies long before the arrival of the Europeans. This is because the use of currency was much easier than continuously trading goods and food. Civilizations often chose things that would not spoil, with gold being one of the most common forms of currency.

People began to consider currency as a way of paying for services. Most people did not know how to read or write, so a scribe could demand payment with a certain amount of currency for writing or reading a letter or document.

One of the primary problems with money was that its value was often unstable and not consistent across multiple civilizations. Money requires another societal agreement among those who use it. Currency can be anything. Gold used to be popular. Today much of the world's currency is just bits of data. Most people use their money through digital means, whether credit or debit cards, or from a smartphone.

There is another example of a shift in how we view currency today with the rise of cryptocurrency. One reason that it is so unstable is that many people simply do not know how it works, so they have not bought into the new kind of currency. Bitcoin, released in January of 2009, was the first cryptocurrency. A somewhat simplified Bitcoin white paper details what it is and how it works. The author of the white paper is Satoshi Nakamoto, but the name is a pseudonym – we do not know who actually created the currency. It is based on a technology that was first theorized during the 1990s but had not been used up to that point.

Bitcoin is not the only form of cryptocurrency today; however, all cryptocurrencies employ the same technology. It is so misunderstood that many people acquire cryptocurrency as a way of investing instead of as a type of currency. What is notable about cryptocurrency is the potential for it to become the primary currency for all people. It is not tied to any nation; it is strictly a technological currency without any government backing. This makes it more similar to the early currencies because many types of currencies were established and failed. The value of a Roman coin now is as an artifact instead of as a currency (although it was a viable currency long after the fall of Rome because of how vast and influential that empire was). Cryptocurrency is more like another experiment - testing the extent to which humans will accept an intangible idea as valuable.

Chapter 10

Empires

Empires have been a constant in human history for thousands of years, but many vast empires have long been forgotten. When discussed, empires often have negative connotations, yet we tend to speak with some level of awe when discussing particular empires. There have been many types of empires, so it is important to understand the defining characteristics.

1. All empires include a large population that covers many different cultures and regions. They are not made up of a single group of people, even if they are part of that empire. For example, the Roman Empire covered a large portion of Europe, the Middle East, and northern Africa. It included people from many different religions and cultures, from the Germanic tribes to Egypt.

2. The empire's borders continue to grow over time until it reaches its zenith.

Kingdoms have become empires, like the British Empire. However, some empires start with a much less obvious structure, with the Mongol Empire being one of the most unique empires in history.

Empires tend to shift and change because they adopt cultures as their borders push into new areas. When Rome conquered Greece, they adopted the Greek Pantheon, creating a shared history. As the Mongols took over new regions, stretching from the Pacific Ocean almost to the Atlantic, they often left their conquered peoples to govern themselves. Only the British Empire was larger than the Mongol Empire, and it adapted many aspects of other cultures. Both of these empires also affected change within the regions that reflected the values of the core of the empire. This is seen by the way Mahatma Gandhi used the ideals of what the British held up as the pinnacle of civilization to reclaim India's independence.

Empires can generate problems. They tend to force conformity of the subjected peoples, often through violence. They grow by conquering their neighbors. Empires can be challenging to negotiate with, and often treat those they have conquered like lesser humans instead of as equals. It is also nearly impossible to sustain an empire, which is often seen as a sign that empires are an ineffective way of governing.

However, empires also unify people. Over human history, the last 2,500 years have seen the majority of the human population belonging to an empire. The end of one empire has typically led to the rise of another. The Carthage Empire fell as the Roman Empire rose, which was followed by the Byzantine Empire. That just covers a few hundred years around Europe, Northern Africa, and the Middle East. Empires also rose in Asia and South America. Often the belief structures and laws of the older empire played a role in the formation of the one that replaced it. This was necessary to retain the trade and stability that the old empire offered. The new empires often helped to minimize the problems associated with the change, although the capital cities always suffered some of the worst shifts as a new capital city took over the region. Knowledge was lost during the transitions, especially during hostile takeovers, like the ones that happened in Carthage and Rome.

Likely, empires existed long before the first ones that historians and archeologists have documented. Among those first known empires was the Akkadian Empire, which was around 2250 BCE. When the leader of the empire, Sargon the Great, died, the empire dissolved. Neighboring nations began to fight for control of the region. This was one of the earliest examples of the rise of empires and how they influenced different regions. The people in control of the empires tended to treat the populations of new areas as less important. In the early days, this created a sense of unity within the empire and often reduced xenophobia. In making the people of conquered areas part of their empire, they were, in a sense, adding team members to a team.

Each empire has been unique in its own way, even though they have adapted earlier empires and cultures. They have taken different shapes and had different foci, which has made it challenging to define them. There have been several positive and negative components, but ultimately empires have played an important role in human history as they have evolved with the different needs of humanity.

Chapter 11

Enlightenment

Progress and understanding of the world have been slow to develop in the human consciousness, with people having little reason to question these things when they were struggling to survive. About 500 years ago, people began to question the world around them. Up to this point, people used stories, legends, religion, and fate to explain the world around them. Then people began to question what had always been believed to be true or to ask things that no one had ever considered before.

This was the beginning of the Scientific Revolution. This was only possible because people started to acknowledge that they were ignorant. Some things and events could not be explained through traditional means, or that were not adequately explained based on what people knew. There was a thirst for a better understanding of the world around them, as seen by the works of Copernicus, da Vinci, and

Galileo. It was no longer good enough to simply say that it was the will of a deity or because that was the way things were. People wanted to know why something happened.

Disasters facilitated some of the desire to learn more. For example, the Black Death swept across Asia, the Middle East, Northern Africa, and Europe, and no one was spared. Entire towns were wiped out, members of royal families and prominent clergy died, and nothing seemed to stop the spread. Venice began a quarantine, which seemed to slow the spread of the disease. While people began to recognize that a quarantine worked, they did not know why. Following the Black Death, the reduction in the workforce, coupled with droughts and floods, resulted in less food, perpetuating the downward spiral of death. People looked at the world around them and realized that there had to be an explanation for what was happening. Admitting that they did not know was the start of learning how things worked.

Humans began to establish new methods to test theories to determine how things worked and why. Up to this point, certain thought processes and beliefs had remained mostly static. With the beginning of the Scientific Revolution, humans began to take a much greater interest in virtually everything. The more things people admitted that they were ignorant about, the more they realized they did not know. Science and exploration became one of the driving forces across the globe as people started to look for why things worked and how they could change their own lives. The next 500 years saw a rapid path to progress. The more people understood the more they were able to change the world around them.

Chapter 12

Science

As people realized that they were ignorant, empires were starting to send explorers out to find new paths to riches. The rise of Spain and Portugal and their respective empires saw a considerable shift in the importance of exploration. Initially, Spain and Portugal wanted a faster, more reliable route to Asia because there were many resources there that were in high demand in Europe. Instead, explorers encountered two entirely unknown continents, shocking all of Europe. Greed was a significant factor for their interactions with the native peoples that they found, but over time other European nations would play more significant roles when the two empires waned. When England, France, and the Netherlands saw that North America did not have the same kind of wealth as South and Central Americas, they began to rethink the potential use of the lands. What North America seemed to lack in gold was more than made up for in unique crops and resources.

Naturally, there was far more information that they did not know than they did. Explorers were sent to start settlements and to learn more about the new worlds. Once they crossed the Atlantic and around the southern tip of South America, they set sail in the Pacific Ocean, seeking new lands.

These trips required more than just people who were able military men; they needed scientists, botanists, and other men of science to understand the different lands. Cartographers provided vital information about the places they went. With so much room to expand the European Empires into unknown regions, the Scientific Revolution was able to help them survive in the new lands.

The benefits to science are undeniable, but there was an inverse effect on the indigenous populations everywhere the Europeans went. Genocide and illness decimated the people the Europeans encountered, except in Asia. Asians and Europeans already had some basic knowledge of each other's technology, though European technology did advance faster during the first part of the Scientific Revolution (Asia experienced a similar cognitive shift, resulting in products like gun powder). The interactions with native peoples in other lands taught the Europeans a lot about the world around them, which gave them some advantages. Many of the nations in Asia also did not demonstrate a similar interest in exploring the world the way the Europeans did. Asians preferred to learn about the world closer to home, coming across many of the same scientific findings, without the same focus on the military and exploration. However, they were savvy enough to know how to repel most of the Europeans' attempts to invade their lands.

Exploration gave the European Empires an eye-opening experience into the world, and they were able to begin positing theories about the evolution of humans – starting with native peoples in lands that the known world had not known existed. Perhaps the best-known example of a scientific advance is illustrated by the trek of the HMS *Beagle*, which carried the young scholar Charles Darwin into lands where no people had lived. He began to theorize on how species had evolved so differently in the new lands, resulting in his theory about the survival of the fittest. He was not the only European scientist to offer this theory, but he became the best know because of his publication, *The Origin of the Species*. It was one of many new ideas that resulted from exposure to new lands and peoples. Humans were further forced to question what they had believed. The more they questioned, the more they began to believe that nothing was impossible. That combination of belief that anything was possible and a desire to explore led to flight, and, eventually, people walking on the moon.

Chapter 13

Capitalism

Capitalism has an interesting place in world history because greed has traditionally been viewed as a bad quality for a person to have. What drives capitalism is the possibility to improve a person's or country's circumstances through growth and profits. Empires acquired money through conquering other lands, but the birth of capitalism made them start looking for other profiting methods when it became clear that traditional wealth limited growth.

The potential to profit led to the rise of increased interest in loans and investing in explorers. While they did not' expect to find gold, European empires began to look for ways to turn resources into profit. The growth of products like tobacco in North America had far more potential to bring in continued profits because the crops could be grown every year. Once gold was found, there would not be any more from that same source.

Of course, settlements and agriculture came with some very high risks, including death. This began to change how people viewed greed and a desire for wealth. More people who were born to more impoverished families were able to start to profit, creating a sense that things were moving more toward equality. Capitalists looked for potential profit sources and were willing to take risks because they seemed to have less to lose. They were also much more likely to spend any money they acquired because they reinvested their earnings in their endeavors. The only way to grow was to put whatever money a person earned back into their business.

As a result, financial institutions changed significantly. They were more willing to offer loans to empires in the hopes of seeing high returns on those loans. Capitalism created possibilities that had previously not existed. This fueled science, technology, and exploration, building on what the Scientific Revolution had started. This does not mean that capitalism is not without some significant flaws. There is a sense that something did not work simply because it did not deserve to work, which has actually delayed progress in many areas. It can also be used to justify unethical behaviors because it is up to the market to decide if something unethical is acceptable.

Like any other ideologies, when properly cultivated, capitalism has much potential to do good. However, it is important to remember that it is fueled by greed, something that does tend to play to the worst traits in people. Healthy capitalism requires a delicate balancing act.

Chapter 14

The Industrial Revolution

Between the time they first started working on Earth and 1600 CE, only a few revolutions resulted in significant changes to how we behaved or to the tools that we used. Since the Scientific Revolution, humans have essentially been in a perpetual state of revolution - with a few lulls. If the Scientific Revolution made people start to think about how little they knew of the world, the next major revolution, the Industrial Revolution began to search for ways to use the knowledge that they had gained to improve how people got from place to place. This was important because of how far the species had spread across the world (largely as a result of empires) and the growing unification of people everywhere.

The rise of capitalism had created what seemed like an infinite potential for prosperity, but after more than a century of prospering, a new problem arose; there was a finite amount of resources. When those resources ran out, it would be nearly impossible to prosper. Scientists had made enormous strides in understanding the world around them, and they began to consider better locomotion methods than the traditional means. Traveling long distances by land required horses. Traveling across the ocean meant being at the whim of the weather because rowing for months simply was not a viable option. The primary form of energy in the home was fire, which was used for cooking and warming homes. Wood was a finite resource, and the amount of time it took to grow a tree made this an unsustainable source of energy. Scientists figured that there had to be a way of harnessing energy sources beyond wind, water, wood, and animals to handle the growing energy needs.

The first significant change in energy sources came with the realization that, by burning coal, water temperature could be controlled for long periods, and by keeping the water hot, humans could use the steam as a way of sustaining energy. Without this energy source, there would be no trains, cars, planes, or rockets today. New machinery was created to better mine coal, which made people rethink other industries because now they could use steam energy to power large machines instead of relying on dozens to hundreds of workers.

Humans began to consider just what could be a potential source of energy. Then one man began to question what made energy. This momentous shift in thinking about energy is the grain that eventually led to the calculation of the famous equation, E=mc2, by Albert Einstein. This has made it possible to determine just how to turn something from a source, such as oil, coal, or radioactive metals, into energy.

Initially, coal was effective, but it soon became apparent that it was also a detriment to human health. The combustion engine was the answer to this problem, along with the burning of petroleum as the primary source of energy. The first combustion engine was patented in 1872. By the end of the century, homes began to have electricity run into them, but only privileged people could afford it. After 120 years, electricity is an expectation in homes around the world.

The Scientific Revolution began around 1543 and ended by the end of the 17th century. The Industrial Revolution began around 1760 and ended around 1840. Some historians have identified several different Industrial Revolutions.

1. The first saw the rise in the use of steam and water to power devices and machines.

2. The second began around the discovery of electricity and its use to power large machinery. Mass production began to be a viable option for meeting the growing demand for a wide variety of products.

3. The third included the rise of automation and information technology. This includes inventions like the telephone.

4. The fourth one is currently happening around us now and is called the Technological or Digital Revolution.

Chapter 15

The Digital Revolution

Some people call the current revolution the Technological or Digital Revolution instead of the Fourth Industrial Revolution. Since the beginning of the Industrial Revolution, humanity has changed more rapidly over each decade than it has in several hundred years up to that point. There has been no point in history where the world has changed so remarkably over a single century as it has between the turn of the 20th and 21st centuries. Apart from noticeable external changes such as clothing and hair styles, life did not undergo many significant changes before the beginning of the first Industrial Revolution. However, the advances in technology by the beginning of the 20th century, coupled with a much better understanding of the world, allowed for people to start using that knowledge to change their world significantly. Ships became larger, the Wright Brothers finally succeeded in building a flying machine, and the telephone all prepared the world for some of the changes that would make humanity nearly unrecognizable.

However, it was the latter half of the 20th century when human behavior became heavily influenced by the technology they had created. Computers made it possible to do a lot more in a shorter period of time. By the end of the 20th century, mobile phones were starting to become affordable. Within a decade, technology had advanced so rapidly that children could not imagine a world without smartphones and the ability to communicate with anyone anywhere. This had an incredibly unique effect on people – something that was impossible without technology – they could stay in touch with virtually anyone without ever leaving home.

Between television, computers, and video games, people have become more sedentary than at any other time in human history. There is an anonymity that is possible with an online persona that was impossible prior to the end of the 20th century. People had to interact with each other in person; while it was possible to lie, body language and facial cues make it easier to tell when someone is lying. Online communication can even remove vocal cues through services like email and instant messaging.

Technology has completely changed how humans behave and what they are now capable of doing. We can quickly learn virtually anything through quick searches online (though it sometimes still requires hours since anyone can post anything online, leading to a problem with misinformation). Videos show us how to do things that 100 years ago required specialists to do. The Covid-19 pandemic showed that it was possible for people in nearly any position (except the service and a few other industries) to work from home. This was impossible at any other previous point in history since currency became an acceptable form of payment.

The potential of technology makes it impossible to accurately predict where humans will be in a quarter of a decade. Too many different aspects of human life are so closely tied together now that changes to any one industry often ripple through all of them.

Another significant change because of technology is in the human lifespan. When Homo sapiens began to roam the Earth, life expectancy for those who banded together was higher than for those who lived alone. However, technology has advanced healthcare so that medical intervention can extend a person's life until long after a severe bodily trauma has occurred, whether that trauma is from an external (such as a car accident) or an internal source (such as a heart attack). This has further changed human behavior and changed the workforce around the globe as there are far more older people now than at any other point in sapien history.

These significant shifts in behavior, lifespan, and ability to learn will likely cause even more rapid changes to the species in the future.

Chapter 16

Familial Structures

The ease with which people can now communicate and travel has changed humanity on a fundamental level – the family. Throughout much of human history, people have remained close to their families, with extended families usually living within easy traveling distances. The age of discovery saw a significant change in the family structure as people moved to new continents to find better opportunities. It was understood that this was risky, and that family members could die. Today, families move to different cities, states, provinces, or continents because they can. This could be a component of wanting to improve their lives, but it is about as common that people move out of curiosity or a desire for change. There is not nearly as much risk associated with this change, and people can still contact their families every day.

This has led to a breakdown in families and reduced social support structures. Virtual connectivity does not provide the same stability and support that people used to have when they continued to live near their families.

Instead of relying on family, people have become more reliant on governments to fill the roles that families used to fill. Governments are responsible for managing vast amounts of money that we allow them to collect. This money then goes to the military, regulations, roads, utilities, and all of the basic requirements of daily life. There is outrage when people find out that their politicians use taxes for personal gain - a misuse of public funds with a long and sordid human history. Kings, emperors, and other forms of governing leaders used taxes as they saw fit. It was what ultimately led to the French and Russian Revolutions. If people live without the assistance of their families, the government tends to take on a similar role to the old family structure, which places a certain expectation on the government not to breach agreements.

The weakening of familial bonds also makes us feel a closer connection to our communities, which has led to a rise in patriotism that largely did not exist under monarchs and other governmental systems. Earlier systems tended to benefit the people at the top primarily, so it did not matter as much who was in control of the peasants. It was not necessary to rely on the leaders because most people relied on family for their daily needs. They did not need roads because most of them did not travel often or at all. Education was not a priority; people needed only to know how to farm and tend to their animals. Parents needed someone else to instruct their children as it became more important for people to learn to read (which was possible thanks to the Scientific Revolution resulting in Gutenberg's printing press). Even after they learned to read, parents had to work, leaving them little time to educate their children. School systems became the primary way of educating children, and that meant that there was some indoctrination. Students learn about their nation's history from their nation's perspective, which often helps to form a sense of community based on the nation.

Today, the growing sense of community among the people who live on Earth is doing more to change once again how people identify with others. Being able to talk to people from other nations is making the mentality of "us against them" increasingly harder to maintain. There is also a growing anti-war sentiment. World leaders themselves do not fight in trenches or on battlefields, which can make them seem more callous to the plight of their people who are expected to fight and die for the nation they do not control. They can talk to people who are supposed to be the enemy and see that their lives are not so different, making it difficult to understand why war is necessary.

It is uncertain where things will go from here. Families remain important, but familial support has evolved as people becoming increasingly more connected. It will be interesting to see how people continue to interact with and support each other.

Chapter 17

Humanity's Future

One of the most challenging things to consider is the end of Homo sapiens. We have already seen the end of all the other Homo species, so it is a reasonably safe guess that humans, as we exist now, have an expiration date as well. But how will that happen?

When people speculate, they often think about events like catastrophic natural disasters, aliens, or war that destroys all human life. While there is a probability for all of these (though the chances are very slim for some), the events of history provide the most probable end, including a bit of a twist because of our technological advances.

This is where we can start looking at how humans are trying to create artificial intelligence, or AI. Science fiction writers have been predicting that humanity would be killed off by the AI we create. That is perhaps possible, even more likely than the other scenarios, but it is still not likely as it is currently impossible to create the kinds of AI that could accomplish humanity's annihilation. If this happens, it is a long way in the future as humans are not focused solely on AI, and some of the current best technical minds are reluctant to move it forward. There is a certain degree of caution with AI because we understand a number of the potential risks.

There are two roughly equal possibilities in their probability. The first is that we will evolve to the point where humans have too few similarities to be considered Homo sapiens any longer. Just like early Homo sapiens were almost certainly able to procreate with other Homo species, particularly Neanderthals and Homo erectus, Homo sapiens may disappear in the same way as our predecessors.

The other likely scenario is tied into the Gilgamesh Project, which is, essentially, humanity's current bid to stop dying. There are certainly benefits the more we learn about genetics and human anatomy, but there are risks that we cannot understand so early in the science. It is possible that we could engineer our own destruction by tampering with our human genetics without having the necessary understanding to do it safely.

The other way the Gilgamesh Project may bring an end to Homo sapiens is through artificial components. People are already accepting of artificial parts being added to the body, or machines that keep us alive. In this scenario, it is projected that people become cyborgs, something that many people already are by the most technical definition of the word. Just like genetic tinkering could change our most basic components rendering us inhuman, replacing our biological components with artificial parts to avoid death makes it difficult to continue to call us Homo sapiens. We may not be able to pass artificial parts on to our children through genetics, and we will likely become dependent on the conveniences of bionic and electrical components, and in doing so, we could arguably become less human.

Considering how people will end is an intriguing, if morbid, exercise, but history has probably shown us our end, and it is not nearly as dramatic or tragic as we consider it to be. Odds are, Homo sapiens as we are today will cease to be, and we will be replaced with the next Homo species.

Conclusion

Homo sapiens have been around for hundreds of thousands of years, and we were not the first ones in our class, just the latest one. We have been far more active in changing our lives than any other animal on the planet. Humans are not the only animal that plays – many mammals engage in play – but we are the only animal that actively looks to change our lives in a way that seems to go against nature, instead of waiting for evolution to take its course. We believe in things that have no substance, from religion and government to currency and liberty. This does not mean they are not real, but they are abstract and mind-dependent, and if we stopped believing in them, they would cease to exist. This kind of agreement is unique to humans.

The rate at which we are changing is increasing in a way that makes it impossible to predict just where we will be in 25 years, let alone 100 years. Many things that we take for granted today did not exist, even in science fiction, 25 years ago. The future for sapiens is exciting and promising, but we ought to be careful as we make changes to ourselves so that we do not accidentally self-destruct.

Made in the USA
Middletown, DE
07 September 2020